D0885624

BOYS
TO
MEN

---

*A Handbook
For Survival*

BOYS
TO
MEN

A Handbook
For Survival

Dr. T. Garrott Benjamin, Jr.

Heaven On Earth Publishing House
Indianapolis, Indiana

Boys to Men
Copyright ©1993 by Dr. T. Garrott Benjamin, Jr.
Light of the World Christian Church
5640 E. 38th Street
Indianapolis, Indiana 46218

All rights reserved. No part of this publication may be repro-
duced, stored in an electronic system, or transmitted in any form
or by any means, electron, mechanical, photocopy, recording or
otherwise, without the prior written permission of the copyright
owner. Brief quotations may be used in reviews.

Printed in the United States of America

All Scripture in King James Edition.

Library of Congress Cataloging in Publication Data
Benjamin, Jr., T. Garrott
    Boys to Men

1. Self help   2. Motivation   3. Religious
    I. Title

93-174693
    CIP

ISBN 0-9637171-1-1

CONTENTS

About the Author.. viii

Prologue xii

Chapter One   **When I Was A Child** 1
* Worms or Butterflies
* The Crisis is at Hand
* Racism: An Equal Opportunity Destroyer
* Dexter Manley is *Not* a Dog!
* White Racism is the Enemy
* Things To Remember

Chapter Two   **Respect Breeds Respect** 15
* Boys to Men
* Boom Boxes vs. Computers
* No More Mamma's Boys
* Ambition or Transition
* More than Mustaches and Sideburns
* Things To Remember

Chapter Three   **Going Through It To Get To It!** 27
* Forget the Game, Boys...
* The Triumphant Transition
* You *Are* What You Think...and What You Read...
* What is in *Your* Library?
* Things To Remember

Chapter Four   **Stand Tall, Black Man!** 45
* 25 Things *Real* Men Do
* A Word to Fathers
* Five Keys to Turning It Around
* Who is Connecting with the Children?
* It is Time for a Change
* The Model of the Master
* Things To Remember

Postscript   **The Respect Academy** 63
* The Respect Academy Litany
* A Closing Word
* Partial Bibliography of "MUST" Reading

ACKNOWLEDGEMENTS

Being of Afrikan descent, I am painfully aware that too much of our rich, oral tradition gets "lost, strayed or stolen" unless we write it down. Sermons included. Messages from the pulpit are not just to be preached — as essential as that mode of communication is. They are also to be *read, and re-read.*

So many of our manuscripts have gone to the grave with us, giving us some of the richest graveyards imaginable.

What you are about to read is my first, formal attempt to polish and publish a manuscript generated from a sermon I preached in my own church. My teaching and preaching tapes are being listened to in homes, offices and automobiles (we call it "feasting in the fast lane") all over the world. But somehow, I believe these *writings* will become even more lasting contributions to the liberation of black people in particular, and consequently to human beings at large, regardless of the color of their skin or place of origin.

There are so many people to whom I owe a debt of gratitude, but I would like to start by thanking my most beloved and loving congregation, which over the years has allowed me so much time away from them to make this book and others to follow possible.

Let me thank Taryn Houston-Scott, Billye Bridges, Alice Hord, and Channing Benjamin for their proofreading and suggestions. My thanks also go to my secretary, Pam Dixon, and my friend, Robert C. Larson, for his thoughtful editorial assistance. I also express my gratitude to my sainted grandmother who helped me make the transition from *boy to man,* and now hopefully from heaven's balcony can get some satisfaction from her investment.

To my wonderful wife, Beverly, who allows me the space to grow and the companionship to glow, I also give my thanks. But most of all, my deep gratitude is to a Great God who "sits high and looks low," and has never failed me yet.

T. Garrott Benjamin, Jr.
Light of the World Christian Church
Indianapolis, Indiana

ABOUT THE AUTHOR

T. Garrott Benjamin, Jr. is a native of St. Louis, Missouri and was raised in Cleveland, Ohio by a single parent grandmother. Since 1969, he has been Senior Pastor of the historic 3,000 member *Light of the World Christian Church* (Disciples of Christ), established 1866 in Indianapolis, Indiana.

Dr. Benjamin is both an innovator and a motivator. His burden for young people birthed the first *Respect Academy* for children in the nation, and his burden for souls birthed the *Heaven on Earth* television ministry, and now, the *Heaven on Earth* Publishing House.

His ministry has been featured in the *Congressional Record, Washington Post, Jet Magazine, The Disciple Magazine,* and other national periodicals. He has written numerous articles and sermons that have been published in a wide variety of periodicals and books.

Dr. Benjamin's ministry has also been seen and felt throughout the world through national cable television (TBN, BET and LeSea) and the Armed Forces Television Network. He has preached on almost every continent, and has recently returned from speaking engagements and fact-finding tours in Australia, Cuba and Russia. He continues to be a highly sought after preacher and lecturer. He is as comfortable in the pulpit as he is in the classroom. He has the uncanny ability to "walk with kings, and yet not lose the common touch" when it comes to communicating God's Word.

He is host producer of the longest running public affairs television program in Indianapolis, "Livin' for the City." Dr. Benjamin is a graduate of St. Louis University, in St. Louis, Missouri, and Christian Theological Seminary in Indianapolis where he earned his Master of Divinity and Doctor of Divinity. He was inducted into the Board of Distinguished Preachers at Morehouse College in Atlanta, Georgia, and also holds several honorary degrees. He is married to his beautiful helpmate, Beverly, and has three fine sons.

FOREWORD...

So much has been spoken and written over the last twenty years about the problems and perplexities of our male children moving from boyhood to manhood, particularly our Afrikan American male children, that it is easy to become weary and over-whelmed by this tremendous challenge. Maybe you ask then, why another book on the rearing of male children?

I'll tell you why. I am convinced our problem today is not a lack of knowledge. We know a great deal more than we are willing to act on. The scriptures declare, "...know the truth and the truth shall make you free." (John 8:32)

We have often interpreted that verse to mean that knowledge and knowledge alone would save us. But it is not merely the *knowledge* of truth that saves us, it is our *acting* upon that knowl-edge that sets us free. It is when we move from *knowing to doing* that we see results.

My friend of so many years, Tom Benjamin, in this wonderful volume, presents some new insights on what we already know about the raising of our children. But the greatest contribution this book makes is that in a powerful and provocative way it calls us to action. Tom Benjamin speaks not only to our heads, but also to our hearts. I hope that you will take what he shares in this volume to heart and act upon it.

Dr. Alvin O'Neal Jackson, Pastor
Mississippi Boulevard Christian Church,
Memphis, Tennessee

With a father's love I dedicate this book
to my three sons,
Benjy, Channing and Chris,
who must make the
transition of being *my* boys
to becoming *God's* men!
I love you so much.

Dad

PROLOGUE

Boys to Men. Biologically, the process is reasonably easy to understand and recognize. Everyone knows a boy is born, goes through his adolescent years, and becomes a man. It is a hormonal thing. So simple. But is it, really? How does a boy become a *real* man? How does he develop psychologically, spiritually and mentally? How does he develop the God-given potential that resides deep within his spirit? How does he become the *man* God intends him to be?

In a country that cherishes European values and ideals, how does a little black boy find his way? How does he navigate through the labyrinth of confusion and delusion on his way to becoming a man? It is not easy, especially when so many of our little boys have to go it alone, with few or *no* black male models to follow.

Boys to Men. Of all the subjects for our time, this topic should rivet our attention as much or more than anything else we could address. When this message was first heard on my television broadcast, the response was phenomenal. Hopefully, this expanded, written version of that message will hit you between the eyes, and strike a cord of response in your heart.

You will not see *all* the answers in these pages, but there *are* answers. Some will become obvious as you read. As for other answers, I will rely on your sensitivity and wisdom to discern them for yourself.

I write this book for all my brothers — young, middle-aged and very mature — who are looking for answers, and helping *others* find answers that make sense on this tedious journey of making the transition from boys to men.

These pages are also for my dear *sisters* who are out there trying to make it on their own, while their little boys are *home alone.* Tears fall easily on my notepad as I write these words, because my heart wants to embrace every little Afrikan American boy as my own son. I hurt for the precious, filled-with-potential black boys who may never become real men.

I hurt for boys whose maturity gets mugged
      by materialism.
I hurt for boys who are raped by racism.
I hurt for boys who allow themselves
      to become gutted by greed.
I hurt for boys who contract AIDS
      before they come of age.
I hurt for boys who get into crack
      before they get into the church.
I hurt for boys who get into gangs
      before they get into God.
I hurt for boys who get into hip hop
      before they get into holiness.
I hurt for boys who get into pistols
      before they get into prayer.
I hurt for boys who get into jail
      before they get into Jesus.

I hurt, and I am angry. This book is a piece of my heart, and I share it with you. Please handle it with care and with prayer. I may not know you personally, but I want you to know I love you very much.

Peace after Justice,
TGB
April 4, 1993

"Of the six leading causes of death among
the adult population, black men lead
the list in each category: homicide,
heart attacks, cancer, suicide, strokes
and accidents. The status of blacks is
beyond the endangered species category."

Madhubuti

"We must learn to live together as brothers,
or perish as fools."

MLK

"We either hang together, or we hang *one at a time*. We have been there, done that, and we did not like it. So there must be another way." TGB

CHAPTER ONE

When I Was A Child...

While we all have differences we could talk about, shout about, argue about, and disagree about, there is one thing we all hold in common — one common denominator. We were once *all* children. We might have grown up in different parts of town, in different kinds of houses or apartments, but we were *all* once boys and girls. Our backgrounds may be as diverse as the colors of autumn, and as varied as the sands of the sea, but we were *all* once children. Regardless of our outward or inward circumstances today, we were once *all* children. The Apostle Paul was once a child, too, and he was *man* enough to admit it in one of his letters of advice and admonition to the church at Corinth. Here is what he wrote to that first century church that has an amazing resemblance to the church entering the uncharted 21st century...

"When I was a child, I spake as a child,
I understood as a child, I thought as a child:
but when I became a man, I put away childish things."

I Corinthians 13:11

This is one of the most dynamic passages in all of scripture because it describes what *ought* to be for our human development in general. As children, we learn to understand life simply. Even though as little ones we may not be able to express it, we still understand love, affection, and caring in our childish way; we also understand what it means to be abused, to be afraid and to be *home alone*. Then, as we grow and develop, we learn how to think, reason, and put two and two together. We slowly begin to figure out what life is all about. What the Apostle is telling us is that we all must *crawl, walk, and then run* — in that order. His main point, however, is that once you are a man, it is time to put away the playthings and get serious about your life. Now, unless you are a child prodigy, you usually learn your ABC's before you start writing great books of poetry. That is just the way it is. That is why the cover of this book depicts the vital stages of healthy growth in a black male child's life — from shaking a baby rattle, to heading off for a day's work at the office.

But what happens when that growth is stunted? What happens to the black child when walls and barriers such as white racism are placed in his way? What happens to an Afrikan American male who remains a *child* emotionally, but wears a suit and carries a briefcase? What happens when a black child never *does* put away childish things?

Worms or Butterflies

Butterflies are beautiful, but they have no choice. They either become butterflies or they die. They might want to remain as hairy, ugly little worms, crawling about in the corners of life, but that is not how they were designed. They *have* to move on. They have to grow. They cannot stay as they were. They either become beautiful, winged creatures, or die!

But people are different. We have a choice. We can choose to grow and glow, or we can turn to rust and then to dust. The pivotal word here is *choice*. Yes, circumstances play a tremendous role in keeping black children out of the promised land of personal potential. But as they grow older, they have a choice. They can go straight, or they can go crooked. They can go to gangs, or they can go to God. However, it is a double bind for these children. How will they ever choose the good things for their lives when what they see all around them is often so bad?

The words of a Holy God, spoken through Joshua, are just as relevant to our people today, "And if it seem evil unto you to serve the Lord, *choose* you this day whom ye will serve...And the people said unto Joshua, The Lord our God will we serve, and his voice will we obey." (Joshua 24:15a, 24)

> "We slaves have come a long way,
> *but we have a long way to go.*"
>
> *Castro to Mandela*

The Crisis is at Hand

As we approach the 21st century, the black community of this nation finds itself in its most desperate dilemma since slavery. We may not be in the fields pickin' cotton as we once did in the old South, but what is happening is just as evil and pernicious, because we are slaves to another order — to consumerism, materialism and tribalism, and the tragedy is that we have almost no consciousness of it.

When I was in Havana, the word was that Fidel Castro had asked Nelson Mandela, upon his visit to Cuba, to thank the Cuban people for their support during his 27 year racist, political imprisonment. Fidel said to Nelson Mandela, *"We* slaves have come a long way." He was right. Neither Castro nor Mandela can forget our past shackles, nor our ongoing bondage — and neither can we. *We* slaves have come a long way, *but we have a long way to go.* But no man is an island, no man lives alone. We either hang together, or we hang *one at a time.* We have been there, done that, and we did not like it. So there must be another way.

Every brother and sister must recognize that this is a clarion call to help save our race in *particular,* and our planet in general. It is a *together* proposition, not the duty of one man, or one woman who has made a commitment for change and put it all on the line.

It is all of us who must get involved.

> "You see I can never be what I ought to be until you are what you ought to be, and you can never be what you ought to be until I am what I ought to be. We must learn to live together as brothers, or perish as fools."
>
> *MLK*

Martin Luther King, Jr. reminded us, "You see I can never be what I ought to be until you are what you ought to be, and you can never be what you ought to be until I am what I ought to be. We must learn to live together as brothers, or perish as fools." That is both *intraracially,* as well as *interracially.* We will never be able to be a brother to another, until we are a brother to each other. That is why we must not forget the big three: faith, hope and love...but the greatest of these is *love* (I Corinthians 13:13).

How bad is it for the black man in this country? How hard is it for black boys to become black men of honor and respect? Haki R. Madhubuti, in his bold, provocative book, *Black Men: Obsolete, Single, Dangerous?* writes:

The world has gotten worse for black men. A young Black man, according to the U.S. Census Bureau has a one in 21 chance of being murdered as compared to a one in 333 chance for a white man of the same age. One of two black young people live in poverty. The black male prison population is over 50%, whereas our population in this country is around 13%. Of the six leading causes of death among the adult population, black men lead the list in each category: homicide, heart attacks, cancer, suicide, strokes and accidents. The status of blacks is beyond the endangered species category.

The news does not get much better. The destruction of black men starts at birth, picks up speed during boyhood, accelerates during their teen years, and comes to its frightful fruition in early adulthood. Too many of our young brothers are either on drugs or selling them. And if you really want to talk about a waste of genes and genius, remember there are *more* black men in jail than in college in this country. And just as you read this last sentence, a few hundred more men were locked behind bars.

> "Lawrence Powell, one of the most vicious of the attacking policemen, when asked on *Good Morning America* how he felt about it all after the state trial, said, 'Rodney King has ruined my life.' White racism always blames the victim."
>
> *TGB*

Racism: An Equal Opportunity Destroyer

Is it bad, or is it bad? The trouble is that not many know how bad it *really* is? Yes, Miami knows how bad it is. Philadelphia knows how bad it is. Chicago knows how bad it is. Detroit knows how bad it is. New York knows how bad it is. Los Angeles knows how bad it is. The Rodney King state trial was American style justice at its worst. Here a black man was beaten mercilessly with clubs, shot with stun guns, stomped on and hit with fists by white cops. Here was a *police riot* on one unarmed black man. Here was a crime *everybody* saw on videotape, and there was not a single state conviction of four white policemen. Lawrence Powell, one of the most vicious of the attacking policemen, when asked on *Good Morning America* how he felt about it all after the state trial, said, "Rodney King has ruined my life." White racism always blames the victim.

In the end, the nation saw four white men pronounced *not guilty* for a crime the *whole world* saw. Yet, in another part of the country, one black boxer would be put in jail for a crime *nobody* saw. How do you reconcile that in the mind of a black child? No wonder black folk say James Baldwin was right when he wrote, "To be black in America is to be in a *constant* state of rage."

But as evil as it is, white racism is not the *only* problem. Black male apathy and irresponsibility are co-conspirators. These are fathers who are more interested in conception than in caring. They want sex without the responsibility. They have not yet learned that fathering a baby does not make you a man, but *being* a father to a baby surely does! Fathers who will not *stay* home or *make* a home are contributing to the corruption and destruction of black boys. If black men are not willing to *stand tall* neither will their sons. It is true: "A man who stands for nothing will fall for anything!"

Dexter Manley is *Not* a Dog!

White racism is usually overt, but sometimes it can be ever so subtle. Either way, it destroys. Here's an example. Not long ago, the respected television journalist and morning TV show host, Charlie Gibson, was interviewing the amazing 275 pound black football player, Dexter Manley about his book. During the interview, Gibson told Dexter that he was a part of his *family*...and he wanted to prove it. Gibson then leaned over and called to his dog. The dog jumped on his master's lap, at which time Gibson said to his *Good Morning America* world about his dog, "I want you to meet Dexter Manley Gibson."

I wrote to Gibson immediately, stating my outrage at his unconscionable racial insensitivity. He wrote me back and said he was "dismayed at my outrage." Well, I am dismayed at his dismay. Can his letter to me — which was *not* an apology — in any way *fix* what was *broken* at that moment in a black boy's mind?

> "In the psyche of a black child there is precious little difference between the vicious beating of a Rodney King and the emasculation of a Dexter Manley. The result — *and* the insult — are the same."
>
> TGB

8

Comments like Gibson's knock yet another corner off the self-esteem of black boys and black men — and white people do not even *see* it. In the psyche of a black child there is precious little difference between the vicious beating of a Rodney King and the emasculation of a Dexter Manley. The result — *and* the insult — are the same.

White Racism is the Enemy

> "America recognizes white racism,
> but has not repented of it. Instead this nation
> blames the victim." TGB

What encourages the destruction of the self-esteem of black boys is *white racism* not black reaction to the actions of whites. And when I speak of white racism I'm not talking about white *people*. Jesus taught us to hate the sin and love the sinner, and if that is not our approach to the problem then we sin just as grievously in the process. In all fairness, it is not white racism alone, as pernicious, insidious and vicious as it is. In fact, white racism must be regarded as a *co-conspirator* in the process, the other *culprit* being those black males who choose to live a life of irresponsibility, inaction and apathy, not even accepting the opportunities that *are* available.

Still, we in the black community would be remiss if we did not demand that the demon of white racism be named, admitted to and confessed by our white brothers and sisters. Then, and only then will healing ever come to America. Our nation recognizes white racism, but it has not *repented* of it. Instead, America is caught in a cycle that continues to blame the *victim*.

Even the sought-after Oscar is lily white for all his *gold* appearance. What do you think it does to the spirit of black children when, during the 1993 Academy Awards, they saw only *one* black person *nominated* among 25 categories?

> "Is it also not important to the Hollywood *elite* that black folk in this country buy almost 50% of the theatre tickets? Don't white folks get it? Yet? Hollywood...Come on, at least see *green* if you are too blind to blink at black!"
>
> *TGB*

Yes, there were blacks on the show, but it was the same old *song* and *dance* routine. Do those folks not get it? Do they not yet know that blacks are making a contribution to the world of film? Is it also not important to the Hollywood *elite* that black folk in this country buy almost 50% of the theatre tickets? Don't white folks get it? Yet? Hollywood...Come on, at least see *green* if you are too blind to blink at black!

> "God wants us to celebrate life, but if the white man keeps his foot on the black man's neck, neither one of them can celebrate. The white man, too, is bound by his own racism. The sooner this is learned, the better off we all will be."
>
> *TGB*

What most people do not realize is that racism is an equal opportunity destroyer. No one gets off on this one. Blacks, whites, browns, yellows and reds are suffering because of white racism. It destroys everyone, *including* white people in the final analysis. Those who are not destroyed are held captive.

God wants us to celebrate life, but if the white man keeps his foot on the black man's neck, neither one of them can celebrate. The white man, too, is bound by his *own* racism. The sooner this is learned, the better off we all will be.

We are losing our best and our brightest brothers and sisters to murder, materialism and the "me-first" mentality of our age. If our anger does not get us killed, then AIDS is going to do it, or jail, or jealousy, or self-hate and self-destruction.

That is why we are *not* going to focus on the *impossible,* but the possible. We are talking more than *problem* here. We are talking *solution.* Thank God for the encouraging, uplifting words of Jesus, recorded for us in the Gospel of Mark, verse 23: "...If thou canst believe, all things are possible to him that believeth." If we are going to make it as a race, let us move from dope to hope... from shirking to working...from having a baby to *taking care* of a baby...from self-conceit to self-esteem. The Chinese say that a journey of a thousand miles (in the original Chinese the unit of measurement is *li,* approximately one-third of a mile) begins with a single step. For us, that step is *respect*...respect for ourselves and for others. Let the serious work begin!

> " '...If thou canst believe, all things are possible to him that believeth.' If we are going to make it as a race, let us move from dope to hope...from shirking to working...from having a baby to *taking care* of a baby...from self-conceit to self-esteem. The Chinese say that a journey of a thousand miles begins with a single step. For us, that step is *respect*...respect for ourselves and for others. Let the serious work begin!"
>
> *TGB*

THINGS TO REMEMBER

1. I will tell my black boy child — and/or any other black male child — how beautiful and special he is. I will do this every day, and every chance I get — in the street, in the store, in the home and from the heart.

2. (To Sisters) I will not put down the father of my son. My son cannot stand one more negative image of a black man.

3. When I speak to people, I will look them in the eye, hold my head high and believe in my heart that *I, too, am somebody.* I am God's child!

"We do not have to agree,
but I must respect you,
and you must respect me!"
TGB

CHAPTER TWO

Respect Breeds Respect

"**D**o not fidget. Stand straight. Look people in the eye when you talk to them. Say, 'Yes sir' and 'No ma'am.' Take your hands out of your pockets. Do not mumble. Respect other people. Respect yourself. Say, 'Thank you.' Say, 'Please.' Give me a firm handshake. Say, 'We do not have to agree, but I must respect you, and you must respect me.' "

This is what we teach black children each quarter at Light of World Christian Church's Respect Academy in Indianapolis. There is no question that urban Afrikan American children are responding to what they are learning at the Academy.

Why do we make the Respect Academy a priority? Because it speaks to the solution. And there's another reason: there is not much time. Every day we lose a child to the enemy that is holding this "heaven on earth" hostage, a part of all of us is ripped away. There is not much time to help our little girls become women of virtue and excellence…and there is not much time to help our little boys become men. Dr. Benjamin Mays, the late, great President of Morehouse College used to say, "We only have a minute. Only sixty seconds in it." Question is, how many minutes are we going to have left to put all this together? Nobody knows.

> "We should all adopt the Afrikan proverb: 'It takes a WHOLE village to raise a child.' "
>
> *TGB*

Boys to Men

I Corinthians 13: 11 is worth looking at again…

"When I was a child, I spake as a child, I understood as a child, I thought as a child: but when I became a man, I put away childish things."

…because it is what this book is all about. It is what saving our children, our race, and our humanity is all about. What white people need to know is that this is not just a *"black* thing." White folk must see that we are inextricably bound to each other. If you want to applaud, you need *two* hands.

> "As the saying goes, 'we've come here on different ships, but we're all in the same boat now.'"
>
> *TGB*

If you want to ride a bicycle, you need *two* feet. Yes, you can compromise and *make do* with a bad situation. But we might as well welcome the notion that we're in this together. As the saying goes, *"we've come here on different ships, but we're all in the same boat now."* So to get stuff done right, it would be real smart if we would team up and do things *together*...like work together, pray together, play together, debate the issues together, and sit down at the same table *together.*

Would you not agree this is a good idea? We should all adopt the Afrikan proverb: *"It takes a WHOLE village to raise a child."*

Boom Boxes vs. Computers

However, unless an Afrikan American male has made an emotionally and psychologically healthy transition from boy to man, he is not going to know what to do if he *does* ever arrive at the table. That is why our mandate is to find, create, discover and improvise to help bridge our boys' transition to responsible, accountable manhood by whatever means necessary.

> "We can no longer afford to match black boys with boom boxes against white boys with computers."
>
> *TGB*

We can no longer afford to match black boys with boom boxes against white boys with computers. Yes, we still have the dream for our boys and men, despite the tribulation. But, look at the hypocrisy of this republic. It will not allow us to mention the name of God in the classroom, but it invites preachers, priests, and rabbis to pray in the statehouse, the courthouse and the White House.

These are the same people who have *In God We Trust* inscribed on their money, but are no worse than white-washed sepulchers, filled with dead men's bones, rotten and stinking to the core, using the name of God to cover their corruption and weakness. Brothers and sisters, these criminal elements posing as public servants are messing with our heads, so let us get it straight: let us take God's Holy Name off those unholy things, and cease invoking God's Name in unholy places. But no, they will not do that.

"No man nor woman will be fully mature until the day Christ returns in His radiance and glory. Only at that time will we be changed. As the Word says in I Corinthians 13:10, 'But when that which is perfect is come, then that which is in part shall be done away.' "

TGB

No More Mamma's Boys

Life is a classroom that prepares us for eternity. It is a process. If we ever wonder why we are down here, struggling, crying, weeping and wailing, it is because we are all still in school. We have not yet had the final exam. So there is no reason to feel terrible because we do not have all the answers. No man nor woman will be fully mature until the day Christ returns in His radiance and glory. Only at that time will we be changed. As the Word says in I Corinthians 13:10, "But when that which is perfect is come, then that which is in part shall be done away."

"Rome was not built in a day," and we are not going to solve our problems during some intensive weekend colloquium where we bring all the right people together who say everything right.

But we are still running out of time, brothers and sisters. Let us not *leave* the classroom, because we are all students and the final bell has not rung. It is time for progress, not recess. Yes, man in heaven is a child matured. Are not black boys entitled to some *heaven on earth?* Can't they live a little before they die?

For starters, we have got to do something about these 20, 30 and 40 year-old boys who are still counting on mamma for protection and direction. Black women need to hear this and know it is true. White men fear neither white women nor black women. White men *fear* black men! So do not let the oppressor turn you *against* the black man. Instead, sisters, give your boys the greatest gift they will ever get. Take your apron, cut off the strings, wrap them all pretty in a box, and present them to your sons. Your boys will get the message, and you will be helping them grow a few more inches toward becoming men.

> "What woman does not want a man in her home who can pray, lay hands on his sick child, earn his wages honestly, and walk with his head held high?"
>
> *TGB*

Any woman worth her salt knows how important it is to get her boys to become men. What woman does not want a man in her home who can pray, lay hands on his sick child, earn his wages honestly, and walk with his head held high?

But we need a paradigm shift right here and right now to help make it happen. The Peanuts' character, Charlie Brown, said it best,

"How do I do *new* math with an *old* math brain?" Good question, Charlie Brown. It is not easy. But when it is tough, we have to do it tough. Black mothers must help their men step to the front and take leadership, and help them become the men God meant for them to be.

Ambition or Transition?

Every black boy has a deep-seated ambition to become a man. But *ambition* is not *transition*. Let us say you have the *ambition* to become a great basketball player. So you go sit in the gymnasium night after night, game after game. You eat your peanuts, take notes on your favorite players, yell and scream with the rest of the fans, go home, only to return the next night again to pursue your *ambition* to become a star. But you have a problem? You forgot to go to practice. You maybe even forgot to get hold of a basketball. Ambition without direction can make a black boy lazy and crazy, and that is what is happening to far too many of our Afrikan American young people every day.

Transition is the word we need to look at. In music, *transition* means moving from note to note in a logical, meaningful sequence. In Latin, it means *passing across.* It is something that actually happens. Musical notes do not just sit there *with the ambition* to go to middle C, or B flat. They do it. They *make* the transition.

But to move toward this transformation takes time. It can't happen overnight. Na'im Akbar, in his landmark book, *Visions for Black Men,* hits the nail on the head when he says, "When the person is able to say to his maleness, 'Wait and be still,' then he has come to a new level of human power and effectiveness. Once the mind has become disciplined, the boy is in a position to grow into reasoning."

It is the *transition* to which we must turn our attention and put our efforts. It is going to be painful and slow, but that is the way it is. We can develop a sunflower in a few days, but it takes years to grow an oak. And there is the rub: do we want sunflowers that are here today, and gone tomorrow, or are we willing to do the hard work of foresting strong, sturdy oaks?

> "...a newborn baby is not given wisdom and age merely because one glues on its face a mustache and a pair of sideburns. Monsters are created that way, not nations."
>
> José Martí

José Martí, the Cuban apostle of Independence, referred to this phenomena when he spoke of the need to embrace heritage:

With some people, an excessive love for the North is unwise, but an easily explained expression of such lively and vehement desire for progress, that they are blind to the fact that *ideas,* like trees, must come from deep roots and compatible soil in order to develop a firm footing and prosper and that a newborn baby is not given wisdom and age merely because one glues on its face a mustache and a pair of sideburns. Monsters are created that way, not nations.

I might add: Neither are *men* created that way...

Martí continues...

One must not judge the spirit of a home and the souls who pray and die there by the champagne and carnations on the banquet table. One must suffer, starve, work, love and even study in vain, but with one's own individual courage and freedom. One must keep watch with the poor, weep with the destitute, abhor the brutality of privilege and wealth, live both in the mansion and the tenement, in the school principal's office and basement, in the gilded theatre box, and in the cold, bare wings. These are the things that make a man.

And these are the things that also make a boy *into* a man!

No amount of smoking nor snorting, sniffing nor swearing, wearing X hats and X shoes, driving fast cars, nor making fast money makes a man a man. These are mere shells, devoid of life and meaning, created as distractions by money grubbers for whom the "long green" *is* everything, and black folk mean *nothing*. Do not buy into the scam. It is a dead end!

Men are made from the inside out, not the outside in. It is a process and it is a passage, not a quick fix. But once our boys get on the journey, and feel confident the new direction is taking them where they can make something of their lives, then their hearts will be lifted. They will discover that there will be some blessed hope after all. Because as John, the Revelator, says in I John 3:2, "Beloved, now are we the sons of God, and it doth not yet appear what we shall be: but we know that, when he shall appear, we shall be like him; for we shall see him as he is."

THINGS TO REMEMBER

1. I will remind a black boy today that he is loved and loveable. I will help him see at least *two positive things* each day he is doing to become God's boy, and eventually, God's man.

2. I will demonstrate to my male child *by* my excellent *example* that cheating, stealing or abuse of our bodies is not God's way.

3. I will tell my boys to expect the best in themselves, and I will help them discover it if they have to go up, down, over, around, or even tunnel through until they do.

"What good is it with an "X" on our heads
if we have a "O" on our minds.
Algebraically, X x O still equals O."

TGB

"When these boys become 18 years old,
we will hold a major, pull-out-all-the-stops
ceremony fit for prime time coverage and better
than video soul, in which our culture comes together and
blesses and encourages these young men who
have prepared themselves for this day.
In Africa, it's called the *rites of passage*.
In America, it's called the same."

CHAPTER THREE

Going Through It to Get To It!

Too many Afrikan American boys have never been through the "rites of passage." I speak from personal experience as one who was raised by a single parent grandmother. I was "grandma's boy" and I was proud of it. True, I did not have any real direction or awareness of the *stages* of my emotional development when I was growing up, and when it came to helping me go through my *rites of passage,* my saintly grandmother did not even realize she was giving me what God gave her — *wisdom.* She did the best with what she had — as most single black parents do!

> "Many of us might have been raised by women who did their best, worked their hardest, sacrificed and saved for us, but they were females, not males, and could not be to a boy what a man can be and should be to his son. A woman cannot teach a boy to be a man. It takes a man to do that."
>
> *TGB*

But, I have said it before, and I will say it until Jesus comes...as long as black boys are raised by women, we have a problem. Many of us have been raised by women who did their best, worked their hardest, sacrificed and saved for us, but they were females, not males, and could not be to a boy what a man can be and should be to his son. A woman cannot teach a boy to be a man. It takes a man to do that. In like manner, a father cannot be to his daughter what a mother can be...it takes a woman to do that.

However, it is better to leave the parenting to a single mother than to have an abusive drunk, druggie or derelict as a role model father for our boys. God bless the women who have stood in the gap. We must continue to understand that we are dealing with what is necessary, not with what is always best.

> "When our young men should be moving on to genuine manhood, many still hide behind their mothers' skirts — and too often they end up *wearing* them."
>
> *TGB*

When our young men should be moving on to genuine manhood, many still hide behind their mothers' skirts — and too often they end up *wearing* them. Disturbing research is beginning to show us that some of the alarming rise in homosexuality among blacks seems due in part to women raising boys. Result? Those boys model the only thing they know — or *do not* know — a present female, and an absentee male.

> "Women and children have been abandoned by immature "boys" who happen to wear men's clothes. But they are not really men. They are still wetting the bed, and crying throughout the night."
>
> *TGB*

Women and children have been abandoned by immature "boys" who happen to wear men's clothes. But they are not really men. They are still wetting the bed, and crying throughout the night. These are not men; these are little boys, still sucking on their thumbs, and light years away from taking the kind of nourishment that will help make them the kind of human beings God designed them to be. Brothers, we must break the cycle of this absurd behavior. It is true that boys will be boys, but is it not now time for boys to be men?

Forget the Game, Boys...

Many of our "men" are still playing childhood games. For them, manhood consists of buying and driving the flashiest car, and breaking their eardrums in the process by turning up their car's over-priced, state-of-the-art quadraphonic sound system, whether they have found the money to pay the rent that month or not. Psychologist Na'im Akbar doesn't hold back when he says in *Visions for Black Men*,

Soon we arrive at his 'pad,' and that's what it is — a launching pad with colored lights hanging down from the ceiling. You go to the bathroom and a blue light comes up out of the toilet, and it goes on from the ridiculous to the absurd. These assumed luxuries are not in themselves objectionable. The objection is that these men are often twenty-five, thirty-five, fifty-five, even sixty-five years old, with the priorities and interests of school boys. They are experts at spending, but only earn with minimal initiative. They are more interested in impressing the 'gang' than anything else. Their wardrobes are chosen in preference to the dressing of their minds or even their own futures. They have no major interest in anything or beyond themselves.

What we are talking about here is "arrested development." When a black boy shoots more pool than he reads books, he is in trouble. When our Afrikan American men spend more time playing ball than time spent in the library, they are in trouble.

If we do not learn from the mistakes of our history, then we are all doomed to repeat them. It is high time to call *time out* in this out-of-control game of self-deception, get back to the locker room, and listen to the coach tell us how it is *really* supposed to be. We have got to end the confusion of what it means to be a black man. God knows that those of us who have given every ounce of our effort to the dream and vision for a race of strong, black men will live out our lives looking for answers, and, if we must, will die trying to make a difference in leading *Boys to Men.*

The Triumphant Transition

The youth minister in our church, Preston Adams, is now working with us on the development of a program that provides the *rites of passage* for black boys so they will know each step of the way *what it means to become a man.* When these boys become 18 years old, we will hold a major, pull-out-all-the-stops ceremony fit for prime time coverage and better than video soul, in which our community comes together and blesses and encourages these young men who have prepared themselves for this day. In Africa, it's called the *rites of passage.* In America, it's called the same thing.

Why all this fuss over a few black boys? Well, it's not a *fuss,* and there are more than a *few!* Young Afrikan Americans need to know when and how to make the transition from boyhood to manhood. They need to know that someone cares. They need to know they are not alone in their struggle against white racism. They need to know they are *not* Dexter Manley Gibson! They need to know they were *not* designed to be riot practice for police. One thing for sure: if *somebody* does not do *something* to bring healing, instruction and direction to our black boys, we have the prospects of watching the gains we have made go up in smoke.

This is a life or death struggle for our people, and that is the reason for the blood, sweat and tears we are putting into our *Respect Academy.* What we are doing at the Academy is not the only answer to our dilemma, but is a very good start, because our seven goals for the children who attend are to . . .

1. Enhance moral and spiritual values by
   teaching them solid, ethical principles.

2. Promote love, cooperation, and collaboration in our community by teaching children to respect others.

3. Facilitate intellectual and personal growth by teaching children the value of self-discipline and self-respect.

4. Encourage ethnicity and excellence.

5. Promote culture and Christ.

6. Focus on values and vision.

7. Hold high heritage and holiness.

You *Are* What You Think...and What You Read

My good friend, Dr. Jawanza Kunjufu, is on top of the "education" issue in his book, *Countering the Conspiracy to Destroy Black Boys, Vol. II,* when he asks these hardball questions about *who* is going to provide answers to those black boys who are going to remain ignorant unless someone cares enough to get involved in their lives:

Who is going to teach Black boys to do their homework as soon as they come in from school with the music and television off? Who is going to teach them to be responsible for their actions in school, and for their grades? When are Black boys going to learn to take one toy outside at a time, and always bring it back before bringing in another...Who is going to teach their sons to respect protocol at activities, and to be punctual about time commitments and class schedules?

Carter G. Woodson says, "Control a man's thinking and you control his action." He also said, "leaders are readers." What have you read lately? I hope your intellectual fare goes beyond the pabulum of a TV Guide, the funnies or the sports page. If it does not, here is a bibliography for you to start working on tonight!

Afrocentricity, by Asante

Countering the Conspiracy to Destroy Black Boys, Vols. I, II, & III, by Jawanza Kunjufu

The Isis Papers, by Frances Welsing

Destruction of Black Civilization, by Chancellor Williams

The Mis-Education of the Negro, by Carter G. Woodson

Visions for Black Men, by Na'im Akbar

Coming of Age: African American Male Rites of Passage, by Paul Hill, Jr.

You see, we shall not only *overcome*...we shall also become *informed!* That is a key part of the overcoming! If we are not self-teachers and self-learners, we will go through the rest of our lives miseducated, uneducated and under-educated. That's why we must read as if our lives depended on it. Because they do! However, when it comes to a book that *really* matters, a book that makes an eternal difference, a book that heals the body, feeds the spirit and saves the soul, I have reserved the best until last. It is *The* Book, The Bible, God's Word.

"And ye shall know the truth, and the truth shall make you free."

John 8:32

"Jesus Christ is the same yesterday, and today, and for ever."

Hebrews 13:8

"Call upon me, and I will answer thee, and shew thee great and mighty things, which thou knowest not."

Jeremiah 33:3

"It is the spirit that quickeneth; the flesh profiteth nothing: the words that I speak unto you, they are spirit, and they are life."

John 6:63

"Train up a child in the way he should go: and when he is old, he will not depart from it."

Proverbs 22:6

"He that spareth his rod hateth his son: but he that loveth him chasteneth him betimes".

Proverbs 13:24

The Word of God is the Will of God. If there is anything I want to know about anything — when I'm looking for *real answers* — I go directly to the Word. Man's opinion is arbitrary, but the Word is immutable, unchanging, ever sure, and our guide for faith and practice. Jesus is the Word (John 1:1). That's why we *do* have an answer in this struggle to help young Afrikan

American boys become men, an answer found in the person of Jesus. In Hebrews 13:8 we read, "Jesus Christ is the same yesterday, today, and for ever." It's shoutin' time to know that some things never change.

If you have not taken *The* Book seriously lately, here are a few samples from the Word to help stimulate your mind, and prepare you for what God wants *you* to do to help save our race and help our boys become men. Read these verses with a prayerful heart, and let them wash over your spirit and cleanse your soul...

God's Availability

Call upon me, and I will answer thee, and shew thee great and mighty things, which thou knowest not.

Jeremiah 33:3

God's Comfort

Why art thou cast down, O my soul? and why are thou disquieted within me? hope in God: for I shall yet praise him, who is the health of my countenance, and my God.

Psalm 43:5

God's Discipline

Train up a child in the way he should go: and when he is old, he will not depart from it.

Proverbs 22:6

He that spareth his rod hateth his son: but he that loveth him chasteneth him betimes.

Proverbs 13:24

God's Faithfulness

What shall we then say to these things? If God be for us, who can be against us?

Romans 8:31

God's Promise

Be strong and of a good courage, fear not, nor be afraid of them: for the Lord thy God, he it is that doth go with thee; he will not fail thee, nor forsake thee.

Deuteronomy 31:6

God's Trust

Trust in the Lord with all thine heart; and lean not unto thine own understanding. In all thy ways acknowledge him, and he shall direct thy paths. Be not wise in thine own eyes: fear the Lord, and depart from evil.

Proverbs 3:5-7

God's Thoughts

For my thoughts are not your thoughts, neither are your ways my ways, saith the Lord. For as the heavens are higher than the earth, so are my ways higher than your ways, and my thoughts than your thoughts.

Isaiah 55:8,9

If we would help our boys be men, God's Word must be the "lamp unto our feet and the light unto our pathway" (Psalm 119:105). If we are going to help our boys cross the rivers of difficulty, despair and delusion, we must take our counsel from the Word. We must take it down from the shelf, dust it off and lodge it in our hearts. The Bible has the answers to helping *boys become men,* but it is up to us as a race to make those answers work for us and for the needs of our people. The Word works, but we must work the Word.

What is in *Your* Library?

"But we must read with understanding. We must say it over and over: readers are leaders, and leaders are readers."

TGB

Whenever I go into a brother or sister's home or office, one of the first things I do is check out the bookshelves. Those books, magazines, videos and tapes tell me volumes about a person's interests, attitudes, depth of knowledge, or lack of understanding. Sometimes I do not see a single book. But the *soaps* are going strong. The tragedy is that television has replaced our libraries, and the tube has become a lethal weapon in Satan's arsenal.

What would I be treated to in *your* home if I came visiting? Would there be piles of mental junk food scattered around your living room — comic books, pornography, R-rated videos and lottery tickets. Or would you say, *Pastor Benjamin, come look at my library. I am so proud of it. No, it is not complete, but I am working on it, and I am making progress. Here is my Bible, which I read daily...here is my bibliography of essential black authors...here are my books on our Afrikan heritage...*and so on.

Brothers and sisters, we have got to read, and read, and then read some more! But we must read with understanding. We must say it over and over: readers are leaders, and leaders are readers. If we have not read and *got into our spirits* the significance of the autobiography of Malcolm X, then the "X" on our shirts and caps might be in fashion but we are foolish and out of focus.

Tragically, many of our black youth under 25 did not read the book *or* see the movie because it didn't have *enough* violence or sex. It's the beginning of the end. For many of us, we are all style and no substance. We might look good on the outside, but inside we are little boys, still playing our childish games.

> **What good is it with an "X" on our heads if we have a "O" on our minds. Algebraically, X x O still equals O. Black man, what do you have in your head right now? Black man, do you have enough going on inside to *stand tall?* Remember the words of the Apostle Paul...*When I was a child, I acted like a child, understood like a child, but when I became a man — when I became responsible — I threw away childish things.***
>
> **If we are going to teach our little boys how to become men, there must be a nationwide effort — starting in our homes and in our churches — to help the potential *man inside the little black male child* to stand up and be counted, to be responsible, and to become the real man God wants him to be. It won't happen over night, and it is not supposed to happen over night. We are going to have to go through it to get to it!**

Frankly, this nation needs a heaven sent, earth shaking, sin shattering, devil hating, Holy Ghost revival. If there is any one *answer* to helping boys become men, that is it! But first we need personal repentance from sin. Following on the heels of that personal recognition that we are lost and on our way to hell, we need a corporate repentance, and then a national repentance. Listen to one of the most profound passages in the entire Word of God. But do more than just read these words. Believe God. Trust God. Be that person of prayer and humility...

> If my people, which are called by my name, shall humble
> themselves, and pray, and seek my face, and turn
> from their wicked ways; then will I hear from heaven,
> and will forgive their sin, and will heal their land.
>
> *II Chronicles 7:14*

Lord, may there be healing in this land indeed, and may it begin in me — today, tomorrow and every day until I die. And may our little black boys know what it is like to one day be *real* men who read no book but the Bible daily, hate nobody but the devil totally, and exalt no one except Jesus completely.

THINGS TO REMEMBER

1. When I am introduced to someone, I will offer my own name first, look that person squarely in the eye, shake his or her hand firmly, and smile. When someone asks me, "How are you?" I will stand tall, not fidget, not mumble, not look down, and say, "I am blessed." I am God's child.

2. I will make my own *home* a *Respect Academy.* I will help my black boys understand what it means to love and respect themselves and others.

3. I am black, and I will stand tall, whether I am with my family, or whether I am *home alone.* I will be a responsible, honest, trustworthy person, whether anyone else is looking or not.

"Real men who are single and saved, know there is no such thing as safe sex — only *saved sex*..."

TGB

◆ ◆ ◆

"Virgins can always be fornicators, but fornicators can never be virgins."

TGB

◆ ◆ ◆

"Boys talk back to their parents; men *take care* of their parents."

TGB

◆ ◆ ◆

"Until *you* become a man...you will never help your *boy* become a man. If anything, you will be the biggest barrier to his emotional, spiritual, psychological and sociological development."

TGB

"I want out of the gangs.
I'm 17 years old, and I want out,
but I'm scared, because they hurt you
real bad when you try to get out."

CHAPTER FOUR

Stand Tall, Black Man

If our Afrikan American boys will ever become men, they must be taught *by example* to assume the manly responsibility of throwing away those things that are doing none of us any earthly good. We have probably all seen the license plate frame that reads, *The difference between the men and the boys, is the size, the look and price of their toys.* That is a vicious, venomous lie peddled from the pit of perdition. It's cute, but not correct. The list of what *real men* do is not so easily put into a *pop* slogan. It is too precious, too valuable, almost sacred. Here are just a few of the hundreds of things *real men* do. I encourage you to take pen and paper and expand the list, because it is not meant to be exhaustive, but encouraging and enlightening.

> "Real men get a job and keep a job; they are providers, protectors and priests. Real men are family men. Real men are *faithful* to their wives. They realize if they spent as much time on their wives as they do on their girlfriends, *they would have the wives they were making the girlfriends to be.*"
>
> *TGB*

25 Things *Real* Men Do

1. Real men put away toys and pick up tools.
2. Real men do not just play — they pray.
3. Real men do not just party — they participate.
4. Real men do not just work out — they work!
5. Real men do not just date — they develop.
6. Real men do not just father a baby — they become a father *to* the baby.
7. Real men do not just love them and leave them — but they love them and help them…bless them and hold them, support them and take care of them.
8. Real men respect and cherish women as Daughters of the Nile…as descendents of Eve, an Afrikan woman who is the Mother of all civilization. (This makes racism even more ridiculous, because Black or White, we have the same mother!)

9. Real men take care of their babies...pay their support, and pay it on time, in the right amount, with some extra thrown in.

10. Real men stand on the Promises instead of the promiscuous.

11. Real men call home, and tell their wives if they cannot make it home. They also tell them *why!*

12. Real men, who are married, come home at a decent hour, because they respect their wives and children.

13. Real men who are single and saved, know there is no such thing as safe sex — only *saved sex.* Any sex without the benefit and blessing of marriage is headed for physical and spiritual disaster.

14. Real men open doors, stand up when a woman enters the room, or arrives at the table. This real man always offers the woman his seat.

15. Boys talk back to their parents; men take care of their parents.

16. Boys wear hats inside a building; men remove them out of respect for themselves and others.

17. Boys cuss a mile a minute; men guard their tongues.

18. Boys chase girls; men respect sisters.

19. Men work for their money; boys expect something for nothing.

20. Real men get a job and keep a job; they are providers, protectors and priests.

21. Real men are family men.

22. Real men are faithful to their wives. They realize if they spent

as much time on their wives as they do on their girlfriends, *they would have the wives they were making the girlfriends to be.*

23. Real men do not do cigarettes, alcohol or any other drug. They know their bodies are a sacred gift, a temple of the Holy Spirit, and not a place for sin.

24. Real men know that sex is who you are and love is what you do.

25. Real men never lift a hand to women unless they are reaching to Heaven to bless her.

How do you come out in this *real men* hall of fame? Your answer will tell you something powerful about your present *and* your future.

A Word to Fathers

Brothers, your sons *want* to be men. But they cannot just go to the gym, gaze adoringly into the workout mirror, flex their biceps and quads and say, "Now, there's a real man!" No one becomes a *real* man by substituting shadow and sweat for substance and stability any more than pasting a mustache over the upper lip *makes* a boy a man.

We have to earn our manhood, and we must teach our boys to earn it. *"But Pastor Benjamin,"* you moan, *"my daddy didn't love me. He deserted us, and mamma was left holding the bag, and we didn't feel good about ourselves."* My brother, I am sorry you feel that way about your condition, but it is time to get off the "pity pot" and start pushing your potential.

> "Just because your father failed you, don't you fail your son. Do not use your own dismal past as an excuse to pass it on to your son. Don't you be the one who introduces your boy to drugs. Don't you be his model for stealing, cheating, drinking, and chasing women. Can you imagine your son saying one day, 'My dad introduced me to drugs, alcohol and pornography and pimpin'?' "
>
> *TGB*

Just because your father failed you, don't *you* fail your son. Do not use your own dismal past as an excuse to pass it on to *your* son. Don't *you* be the one who introduces your boy to drugs. Don't *you* be his model for stealing, cheating, drinking, and chasing women. Can you imagine your son saying one day, "My dad introduced me to drugs, alcohol and pornography and pimpin'?"

It is still true: *it is not what is taught that always counts; it is what is caught!* So the question...what is your son *catching* from you? Is he reading your smut literature, the kind you use to stimulate yourself in unnatural ways? Are you the model for child abuse, spousal abuse and sexual abuse? Children *do* what they *see*. And God sees what we do.

If you are doing these things, you can't blame the white man for your problem. You can't blame the welfare system for your condition. Until God opens your eyes, blinded by Satan and sin, you will not see *who* you are or *whose* you are. Until you name your sin and repent of it, (which is more than just saying, *'I'm sorry,'* because we have enough *sorry folk* already,) you will stay in your despair and darkness. Repentance means you turn your back from your sin and walk in the opposite direction. The recognition of bondage is the beginning of blessing.

Until *you* become God's man, you will never help your *boy* become God's man. If anything, you will be the biggest *barrier* to his emotional, spiritual, psychological and sociological development. And it will be your fault.

Five Keys to Turning It Around

"Blessed is the man that walketh not in the counsel of the ungodly, nor standeth in the way of sinners, nor sitteth in the seat of the scornful...For the Lord knoweth the way of the righteous: but the way of the ungodly shall perish." Psalm 1:1,6

It is my hope that you have already begun to sense the need to be more a part of the solution than the problem. I am not saying you are going to make a 180 degree turn by the time you have read the last page of this book. But a victory will be achieved if I can arrest your attention. Use these words as a handbook for your survival. Use them to help a black child become a man and develop his self-esteem. Use it as your primer — a book that states the problem and provides a few answers to move toward genuine manhood for you *and* your sons.

Yes, it is hard work. Very hard work. From ancient times along the great Nile, the cradle of our heritage and civilization, to the challenges that roll hard against the banks of the Mississippi, the Missouri, the Colorado, and wherever else our people live, breathe and have their being, according to Martin Luther King, "Human progress never rolls in on the wheels of inevitability." It never has and never will. *Change* comes only by the tireless efforts of brothers and sisters who are willing to work at the problem and provide a solution for the boys to men dilemma.

> "There are *no bad boys* and there are no *bad men,* just bad *influences.* Do not believe you are bad. You are not. You are good. My grandmother used to say to me, 'Tommy, you be a good boy, and if you are a good boy, you'll be a good man'."
>
> *TGB*

Here are *five keys* to help you get started in the *transformation* of your mind. Remember...

1. There "ain't" no such thing as a free lunch. Our people have always worked by the sweat of their brow, as we did during slavery (that's the last time we had full employment), and it is no different as we approach the uncertainties of the 21st century. If you want to eat, you must work. The Bible is clear on that. II Thessalonians 3:10 reminds us, "For even when we were with you, this we commanded you, that if any would not work, neither should he eat."

2. You do not have to be a remarkable person to *do* remarkable things. The most unremarkable people have done the most remarkable things. You can do it, too — for yourself, and for our struggle as a people. You can move toward manhood because there are thousands of models of other black men who have done it successfully — men who once thought *change* was impossible. God's Word says, "Therefore if any man be in Christ, he is a new creature: old things are passed away; behold, all things are become new" (II Corinthians 5:17).

3. Simply say *Yes* to change. Make a decision and stick with it. Get help if necessary. God will be your strength, and there will be brothers to hold you and support you along the way. Hear the promise: "The Lord is my light and my salvation; whom shall I

fear? the Lord is the strength of my life; of whom shall I be afraid? When the wicked, even mine enemies and my foes, came upon me to eat up my flesh, they stumbled and fell. Though an host should encamp against me, my heart shall not fear: though war should rise against me, in this will I be confident" (Psalm 27:1-3).

4. There are *no bad boys* and there are no *bad men,* just bad *influences.* Do not believe you are bad. You are not. You are good. My grandmother used to say to me, "Tommy, you be a good boy, and if you are a good boy, you'll be a good man." You are blessed, you are black, and you are beautiful. But you must let the Lord Jesus take you by the hand and lead you through the mine fields of sin and degradation that would destroy you. Then, and only then, will you be free from bondage. Let your spirits be lifted by God's challenge in Psalm 1, verses 1 and 6: "Blessed is the man that walketh not in the counsel of the ungodly, nor standeth in the way of sinners, nor sitteth in the seat of the scornful...For the Lord knoweth the way of the righteous: but the way of the ungodly shall perish."

5. Do not take less when you can have the best. Do not settle for the *minors* when you can make it in the *majors.* Quest for the best and keep your eyes on the prize. He who has ears, let him hear the Apostle Paul's words in Philippians 3:13 and 14: "Brethren, I count not myself to have apprehended: but this one thing I do, forgetting those things which are behind, and reaching

forth unto those things which are before, I press toward the mark for the prize of the high calling of God in Christ Jesus."

Who is Connecting with the Children?

Brother Jawanza Kunjufu's book, *Countering the Conspiracy to Destroy Black Boys, Vol. III,* is *must* reading for every Afrikan American. Here is what the author says about the various kinds of *messages* given to black children, and the *quality* of that message.

Gangs, Dealers, and Media	Parents, Teachers, and Concerned Community Citizens
2 to 8 hours spent together. As age increases, involvement increases.	7 to 34 minutes spent together. As age increases, involvement decreases.
They listen *to* each other.	They talk *at* each other.
Immediate gratification.	Long-term gratification.
Materialism, designer clothing, bright colors (large/flashy)	Internal, moral, integrity, honesty
Advocate money via drugs, sports, music, crime and lottery	Money via good education and working hard

Hear Kunjufu's comment on these statistics.

It should become obvious to the reader that we are not going to win against gangs, dealers, and the media with fathers and mothers spending 40 to 45 minutes disseminating irrelevant information to their youth. Many youth tell me that adults in the neighborhood do not even say hello. Many adults in the neighborhood tell me they are afraid of our youth. Isn't it interesting that as our youth become older, they spend more time together, while most adult involvement is on the decline.

It is Time for a Change
From welfare to faring well.

Yes, what Kunjufu says is interesting. But black folks should not find it *just interesting*. We must all see it for the tragedy that it is — the criminal act of irresponsibility that is keeping our children from becoming men. It is time for a change...

- From non-commitment to commitment
- From irresponsibility to responsibility
- From no respect to *show respect*
- From dope to hope
- From drinking to thinking

- From lust to love
- From shackin' to building relationships
- From taking to giving
- From shirking to working
- From spending to saving
- From self-conceit to self-esteem

That is the transition from boys to men. It is time for a change...

- From being cool to staying in school
- From shucking and jiving to soaring and flying
- From being loud to being proud
- From hanging out to hanging in
- From "baby's got back" to baby's got brains
- From putting folk down to lifting folk up
- From renting to buying
- From consuming to producing
- From material things to things that matter
- From being bitter to doing better

That is the transition from boys to men. It is time for a change...

- From being racist to being racial
- From *other* domination to self-determination
- From imitation to building a nation
- From depending on parents to depending on the power in *you*

- From welfare to faring well
- From trying to be white to being black
- From America to Afrika

That is the transition from boys to men. It is time for a change. If we do not make the transition, God will call it *sin* because "all unrighteousness is sin." Hear the Word of the Lord in Proverbs 14:34: "Righteousness exalteth a nation: but sin is a reproach to any people."

The Model of the Master

"To be great, you must become a servant. You have to help somebody. You have to give a cup of water in My name. You have got to touch people and bless them. You have got to give back. As my buddy, Jesse Jackson, says, 'The blessed of us must help the rest of us.'" TGB

When we look at the life, ministry and personality of Jesus of Nazareth, we see in our Savior the *master model* of maturity and manhood. When He was a little boy, He went to the temple as was the custom. What was *not* the custom was how He confounded the folk who considered themselves the great authorities on the law. Experiences like these helped Him grow in wisdom and stature with both God and man.

But as He became a man, even the Son of God had to throw away childish things. Why? Because He knew we would need a model for our own manhood. Now, hear what He said, because it is what we need to have stamped on our spirits and sealed in our hearts: *To be great, you must become a servant. You have to help somebody. You have to give a cup of water in My name. You have got to touch people and bless them. You have got to give back.* As my buddy, Jesse Jackson, says, "The blessed of us must help the rest of us."

"At age 33, Jesus, the one with 'feet like burnished brass and hair like wool,' went to the cross and died for black people. When He was buried, He was buried for black people. And when He rose, He rose for every Afrikan and Afrikan American who ever lived and who will ever live! As the hymn writer says, 'Because He lives, I can face tomorrow. Because He lives, all fear is gone...' "

TGB

At age 33, Jesus, the one with "feet like burnished brass and hair like wool," went to the cross and died for black people. When He was buried, He was buried for black people. And when He rose, He rose for every Afrikan and Afrikan American who ever lived and who will ever live! As the hymn writer says, "Because

He lives, I can face tomorrow. Because He lives, all fear is gone…" Right now, anyone who is holding back a little black boy when he ought to be becoming a man, will not make it until he goes the way that Jesus went. Our people and our culture have got to go through the valley just like Jesus did. We still have got to meet the trouble, and we have got to shake hands with the tribulation. The Gospel calls us to the "way of suffering." There's no cheap grace. No easy Christianity. No express elevator to the top. It's the way of the Cross, but it's also the way of the Crown.

> "Success comes in CANS — *I can, I can, I can, I can do it!*"
>
> *TGB*

It is not a game, this going from boys to men. It is a responsibility, a position, a condition and a transition. It is time to make the change…and today is the day to start. Success comes in CANS — *I can, I can, I can, I can do it!* And to show you it *can* be done, I want you to meet one little brother who had the courage to put it all on the line.

Anthony decided to follow Jesus, and go from being a hood to being a member of God's brotherhood. I met this young man while speaking at Life Focus '93, an interracial and interdenominational crusade for Christ in Memphis, Tennessee, where 1,000 young people got saved in *one* night.

After the service, Anthony came up to me and said, "Dr. Benjamin, I got saved tonight. I feel great. I feel new. I want out of the gangs. I'm 17 years old, and I want out. But I'm scared, because they hurt you real bad when you try to get out."

I said, "Anthony, tell them you are already out of the *old gang,* and now you belong to a *new gang,* the 'Jesus gang.' Invite them to meet Christ and to go to church with you. That's your best defense and your greatest witness." Paul says, "...Resist the devil and he will flee from you." (James 4:7)

What about you? Are you ready to join the *Jesus gang* along with young Anthony? Are you ready to take some of the answers found in this book and turn your life around? The challenge is in *your* hands, and the choice is up to you. Will you leave the emotional playground of your past and plant your feet in the arena where the *real* men live? It is my prayer, my brother, that you will. Make the change. Let your life be re-arranged. Put the Master in charge of your life. You've got to serve somebody. Why not serve the Lord?

"When I was a child, I spake as a child, I understood as a child, I thought as a child: but when I became a man, I put away childish things."

Let me say it another way...

THINGS TO REMEMBER

1. I am a remarkable person, capable of doing remarkable things. With God's help, and the encouragement of my brothers and sisters, I *will* become a man, starting today!

2. I will do more than party. I will participate. I will no longer be a boy, expecting "something for nothing." There is room at the top, but I won't get there on an express elevator. Hard work plus sacrifice and prayer equals results.

3. My mind is a pearl. I can learn anything in the world. I am a child of the King. I can do anything.

"Bite off more than you can chew and chew it.
Do more than you can do and do it.
Hitch your wagon to a star,
take a seat and there you are!"
TGB

POSTSCRIPT

It's no secret that gangs, violence, drugs, lack of self-respect and lack of respect for others are destroying our nation's children. But what *may* be one of the best kept secrets in this country is the Respect Academy, which I founded and serve as Head Master at Light of the World Christian Church in Indianapolis, Indiana. We can now say with certainty that any church, any home, any school can make a powerful impact on our children. It only requires the desire to take "boys to men."

The Respect Academy teaches children ages 6-12 fundamental *spiritual, academic and social principles* that enhance their *self-esteem* and *respect for others.* The *Rites of Passage* program, (ages 13-18) an extension of the Respect Academy, places its emphasis on a boy's *rite of passage* (an Afrikan tradition) to the world of adulthood, helping him make the transition from "boy to man" through disciplined instruction. Our *Boys to Men* program is a one-on-one mentoring program at Arlington, a local high school with which we formed a continuing partnership, and is also an extension of the Respect Academy. We enjoy the total support of a powerful principal named Jacqui Greenwood who loves God and children with a sacrificial love. And when I get through with this book, the "bottom line" is still love…God's love, tough love, but God's love nevertheless. Every six weeks, we take 50 black men into a local community high school named Arlington where we mentor 50 black boys. We go over their grades with them, and help them work through their many male and school issues. More than anything else, God is using a black adult male presence in this program to make a difference in the lives of boys who otherwise would be on the streets, in the gangs, and lost forever.

The Respect Academy is a *long-term* solution to the gangs and violence problem that is assaulting cities and towns throughout this country. Key elements in the program are the teaching of personal discipline, courtesy, hygiene, self-respect, self-esteem, values, spirituality, and cultural heritage.

Black children are particularly at risk because of the peer pressure to join gangs. The lessons taught at the Respect Academy help young children withstand this pressure, and give them an alternative to a life of violence and pain they will surely encounter on the streets.

The Respect Academy seeks to be an answer to our problem. The most wonderful part is that *anybody who cares can do it.* All it takes are people who are willing to "step up to the plate," and turn their values into vision.

The work of the Academy, while not widely known, is beginning to be recognized for the force it is fast becoming.

Episcopal Evangelist John Guest, originally from Liverpool, England, and I addressed 12,000 souls at Life Focus '93 in

Memphis. Among John's closing remarks he said, "There are two things everyone in this country must do: 1. Accept Jesus Christ as Lord and Savior, and, 2. Go to Indianapolis, Indiana and be amazed at what is happening to the lives of youngsters in Dr. Benjamin's Respect Academy. This program is dramatic proof that there truly *is* hope for our children."

John visited our campus here in Indianapolis, and his first hand report on the Respect Academy was more than encouraging.

On the page that follows I have a special gift for you. Throughout the year I share this Respect Academy *Litany*, which I composed to help lift a child's self-esteem, with more than 800 black children who attend the Academy. It is our hope at Light of the World Christian Church, and the Respect Academy, that these words of support and encouragement will also speak to *your* heart as you use them to help you — or help you help another — make the transition from *boy to man...*

The Respect Academy Litany (TGB)

Praise the Lord! I am somebody!
I am God's child; I am somebody!
I am black, I am beautiful, I am bold, I am blessed...
AND I AM FREE!
We do not have to agree, but I must respect you
and you must respect me!
I respect my history, I respect my country,
I respect the law and the flag,
I respect my teachers and authority.
I respect every religion, race and creed...
I hear what you say, but I respect your deeds.
We do not have to agree, but I must respect you,
and you must respect me.
I respect Mother Afrika, I respect Step-Mother America.
I respect Nelson Mandela. I respect Bishop Tutu.
I respect Martin, Malcolm, Medgar and Elijah Muhammad;
I respect my pastor, and I respect my church.
I respect Frederick Douglas, Harriet Tubman, Nat Turner,
Sojourner Truth, Denmark Vesey, Crispus Attucks, Langston
Hughes, James Weldon Johnson, Marcus Garvey, W.E.B. DuBois,
and Carter G., Booker T, Madame C.J. Walker, and all the rest...
I RESPECT EXCELLENCE...I EXPECT THE BEST!
We do not have to agree, but I must respect you,
and you must respect me!
I am God's child.
I am black, I am beautiful, I am bold, I am blessed
AND I AM FREE!
We do not have to agree, but I must respect you,
and you must respect me!

A Closing Word...

Now that you have read my book, my hope is that you will give Christ your life, if you have not done so already. And even if you have, I pray that God will give you the insight to get a double portion and renew your faith in Christ because Christ *is* the answer. And to all my little brothers and my big brothers, life has taught me one thing for sure: "Only what you do for Christ will last. Only what you do for Him will be counted in the end." Now is the time for repentance, reversal, and restoration but we must "break up the fallow, hard ground". Confess and accept Christ today as Lord of your everything because if He is not "Lord of All He is not Lord *at* all". I want to close by lifting you and your needs to the Lord in prayer...

Father, put Your Hand of Protection on every reader of this book. We know Your Power is in us, on us, and all through us. Open our understanding and renew a right spirit within us. Fill us with Your Holy Spirit until we look like You, think like You and act like You...until we love like You. Help us to stand tall...proud of who we are and Whose we are. We know that the enemy wants to sift our children. particularly, our young black males...as he tries to destroy them and deny them from becoming real men. Right now we are lifting every brother up to You because we know that greater is He who is within us than he who is in the world. Thank you for the Blood that protects and provides. You are doing everything You said You would. Father, thank you for the sisters and the mothers who have stood in the gap waiting for boys to become men. Touch the sisters, O God, with a special anointing of patience, persistence, and prayer. May they not only be willing to stand by their men but also give them the ability to stand up for their men as they lovingly push them to the front where they need to be. O God, we need a fresh anointing. Send Your Power and use this little book as a big blessing in the lives of Your people. It's all for Your Honor and Your Glory. In Jesus' Name, Amen.

TGB

PARTIAL BIBLIOGRAPHY OF
"MUST" READING

Akbar, Na'im, <u>Visions for Black Men.</u> Nashville: Winston-Derek Publications, Inc, 1981.

Hill, Jr., Paul, <u>Coming of Age: African American Males Rites of Passage.</u> Chicago: African American Images, 1992

Kunjufu, Jawanza. <u>Countering the Conspiracy to Destroy Black Boys, Vols. I, II, III.</u> Chicago: African American Images, 1982, 1986, 1990.

Madhubuti, Haki, <u>Black Men: Obsolete, Single, Dangerous?</u> Chicago: Third World Press, 1990.

Martí, José, <u>Tres Documentos/Three Documents.</u> La Habana: Publicaciones en Lengua Extranjera, 1984.

For further information on how to order Dr. Benjamin's books and messages on video and audio cassettes, or to participate financially in this vital ministry to Afrikan Americans through weekly television, tapes, sermons and personal appearances by Dr. Benjamin in this country and around the world, please write or call today:

Heaven On Earth Publishing House

P.O. Box 18088

Indianapolis, Indiana 46218

(317) 547-2273

To Order Additional Copies of

Boys to MEN: A Handbook for Survival
by Dr. T. Garrott Benjamin, Jr.

(for a Ministry Gift of at least $10.00 per book)

Name: _____

Street: _____

City:_____State: _____ZIP: _____

Home Phone: _____Work Phone: _____

Quantity:_____Price: _____

Total Ordered: _____

Handling/Mailing:_____$1.95___

Total Price: _____

Return order form along with check or money order payable to:

Heaven On Earth Publishing House

P.O. Box 18088

Indianapolis, Indiana 46218-0088

Telephone Orders may be placed to (317) 547-2273

☐ Mastercard   ☐ VISA

Account # _____

Expiration Date: Month _____ Year _____

Signature: _____

PLEASE ALLOW 4-6 WEEKS FOR DELIVERY

COMING SOON...

Home Alone Syndrome

"Our children are not just a lost generation,
but they are a *left* generation."

—*TGB*

**A new release from noted author,
Dr. T. Garrott Benjamin, Jr.**